Program Authors

Peter Afflerbach

Camille Blachowicz

Candy Dawson Boyd

Elena Izquierdo

Connie Juel

Edward Kame'enui

Donald Leu

Jeanne R. Paratore

P. David Pearson

Sam Sebesta

Deborah Simmons

Alfred Tatum

Sharon Vaughn

Susan Watts Taffe

Karen Kring Wixson

PEARSON

Glenview, Illinois • Boston, Massachusetts • Chandler, Arizona •
Upper Saddle River, New Jersey

We dedicate Reading Street to
Peter Jovanovich.

~

His wisdom, courage,
and passion for education
are an inspiration to us all.

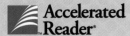

About the Cover Artist
Rob Hefferan likes to reminisce about the simple life he had as a child growing up in Cheshire, when his biggest worry was whether to have fish fingers or Alphabetti Spaghetti for tea. The faces, colors, and shapes from that time are a present-day inspiration for his artwork.

ISBN-13: 978-0-328-48110-1
ISBN-10:   0-328-48110-6
6 7 8 9 10 V011 14 13 12 11

Dear Reader,

Just think about how much you've learned on Reading Street this year! The year is almost over, but we have one last trip. You can use all of the skills and ideas you've learned to help you enjoy it.

This trip will take us to places where animals are building homes and boats, and people are building houses and schools. Keep your thinking caps on. We still have a lot to learn.

AlphaBuddy says, "It's been great working and playing with you. Keep on reading!"

Sincerely,
The Authors

Putting It Together

What are different ways of building?

Week 2

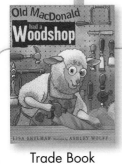

Animal Fantasy · Science
Old MacDonald had a Woodshop
by Lisa Shulman

Trade Book

Unit 6 Contents

Week 3

Big Book

Week 4

Trade Book

Week 5

Big Book

Informational Fiction • Social Studies
The House That Tony Lives In
by Anthony Lorenz

Week 6

Trade Book

Expository Nonfiction • Science
Ants and Their Nests by Linda Tagliaferro

Don Leu
The Internet Guy

Right before our eyes, the nature of reading and learning is changing. The Internet and other technologies create new opportunities, new solutions, and new literacies. New reading comprehension skills are required online. They are increasingly important to our students and our society.

Those of us on the Reading Street team are here to help you on this new, and very exciting, journey.

See It!

- Big Question Video

- Concept Talk Video

- Envision It! Animations

- eReaders

Hear It!

- *Sing with Me Animations*

- eSelections

- Grammar Jammer

Adam and Kim **play at the beach.**

Concept Talk Video

Putting It Together

THE BIG ?

What are different ways of building?

Let's Listen for

Vowel Sounds

Read Together

● Point to the apple. Say the word. Say the beginning sound.

■ Point to the igloo. Say the word. Say the beginning sound.

▲ Find three things that begin with /a/, like *apple*. Find three things that begin with /i/, like *igloo*.

★ Point to these pictures and say the words: *ax, apple, animal*. Do they begin the same? What about *igloo, alligator, umbrella*?

♥ Point to a hat. What sounds do you hear in *hat*? Separate the sounds with me: /h/ /a/ /t/.

Objectives
- Tell how facts, ideas, characters, settings, or events are the same and/or different.

Comprehension

Envision It!

Compare and Contrast

**READING STREET ONLINE
ENVISION IT! ANIMATIONS**
www.ReadingStreet.com

Envision It! | Sounds to Know

Aa

astronaut

Ii

igloo

**READING STREET ONLINE
ALPHABET CARDS**
www.ReadingStreet.com

Phonics

Short *Aa*, Short *Ii*

Words I Can Blend

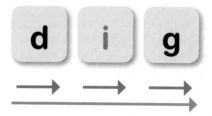

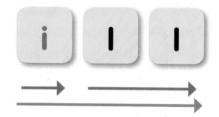

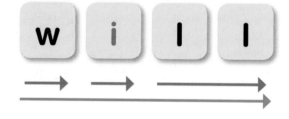

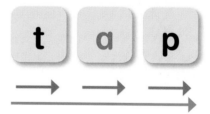

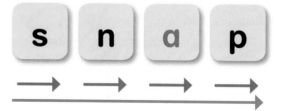

Words I Can Read

here

do

little

with

what

Sentences I Can Read

1. Here is the red bag.
2. Do you like it?
3. Yes, a little red bag is fun.
4. It will go with us on the bus.
5. What is in the bag?

Objectives

● Point out the common sounds that letters stand for. ● Use what you know about letters and their sounds to read words in a list and in sentences or stories. ● Know and read at least 25 often-used words.

Phonics

I Can Read!

Decodable Reader

● Short *Aa*

Sam	can	tap
Cat	pass	gap
nap		

■ Short *Ii*

Kip	big	will
if	dig	Pig
fit	in	

▲ High-Frequency Words

is	little
go	with
here	the
do	what

★ Read the story.

READING STREET ONLINE
DECODABLE eREADERS
www.ReadingStreet.com

If Kip Can

Written by Sara Blumenthal
Illustrated by Ken Ye

Decodable Reader 31

Kip is big.
Sam is little.
Sam will go with Kip.

If Kip can dig here,
Sam can dig here.
Kip can dig. Will Sam dig?

If Kip can tap Cat,
Sam can tap Cat.
Kip can tap Cat. Will Sam tap?

If Kip can pass Pig,
Sam can pass Pig.
Kip can pass Pig. Will Sam pass?

If Kip can fit in the gap,
Sam can fit in the gap.
Kip can fit. Will Sam fit?

If Kip can nap,
Sam can nap.
Kip can nap. Will Sam nap?

Sam can do what Kip can do!

Objectives
● Retell the important facts from a selection heard or read. ● Connect what you read to other things you have read or heard. ● Tell how facts, ideas, or events are the same and/or different.

Envision It! Retell

Big Book

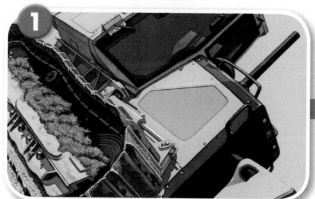

Think, Talk, and Write

1. Think about *Dig Dig Digging.* How is *Building with Dad* like *Dig Dig Digging?*

Text to Text

2. How are a steamroller and a cement mixer alike? How are they different?

Compare and Contrast

3. Look back and write.

Objectives
● Understand that compound words are made up of shorter words.
● Share information and ideas by speaking clearly and using proper language. ● Follow rules for discussions, including taking turns and speaking one at a time.

Let's Learn It!

Vocabulary

● Talk about the pictures.

■ Make compound words with words you know.

Listening and Speaking

● Say a line from a nursery rhyme with a group.

Vocabulary

Compound Words

play **+** ground **=**

playground

book **+** shelf **=** bookshelf

class **+** room **=** classroom

Recite Language

Be a good speaker!

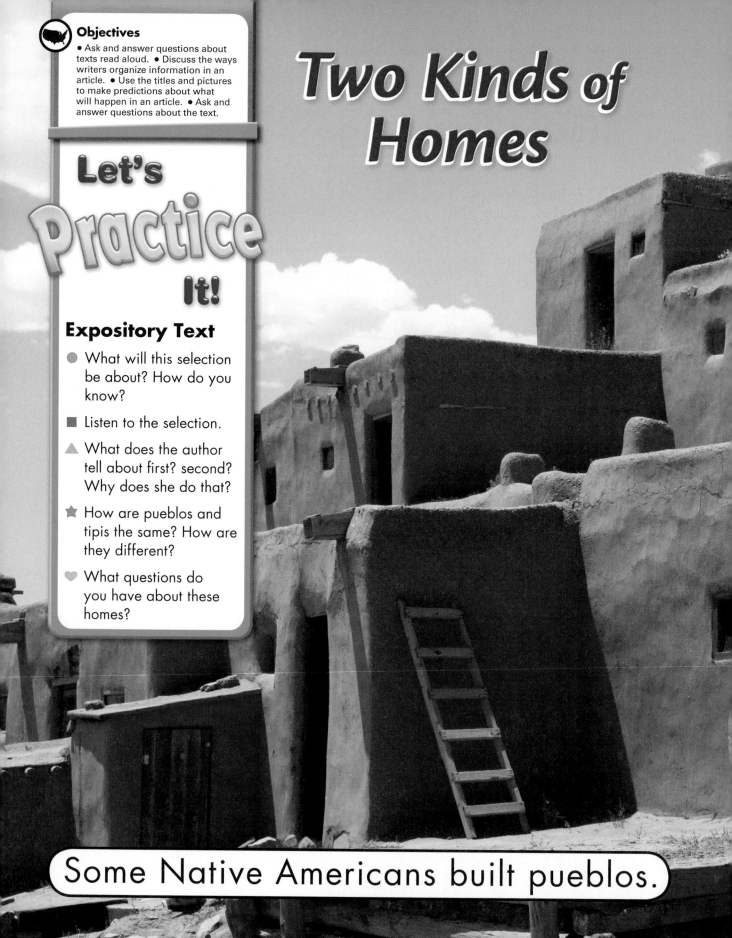

Let's

Practice It!

Expository Text

● What will this selection be about? How do you know?

■ Listen to the selection.

▲ What does the author tell about first? second? Why does she do that?

★ How are pueblos and tipis the same? How are they different?

♥ What questions do you have about these homes?

Two Kinds of Homes

Some Native Americans built pueblos.

Some Native Americans built tipis.

Let's Listen for

Vowel Sounds

Read Together

● Point to the ox. Say the word. Say the beginning sound.

■ Point to the top. Say the word. Say the middle sound.

▲ Find three things that begin with /o/, like *ox*. Find three things that have /o/ in the middle, like *top*.

★ Point to these pictures and say the words: *ox, octopus, otter*. Do they begin the same? What about *cow, operation, fox*?

♥ Point to the top. What sounds do you hear in *top*? Separate the sounds with me: /t/ /o/ /p/.

READING STREET ONLINE
BIG QUESTION VIDEO
www.ReadingStreet.com

Comprehension

Envision It!

Literary Elements

READING STREET ONLINE
ENVISION IT! ANIMATIONS
www.ReadingStreet.com

Characters

Setting

Plot

Envision It! | Sounds to Know

Oo

otter

Phonics

🔄 Short o

Words I Can Blend

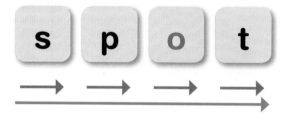

s p o t

→ → → →

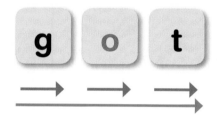

g o t

→ → →

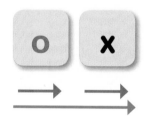

o x

→ →

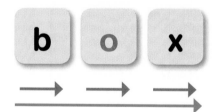

b o x

→ → →

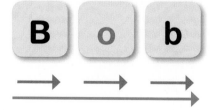

B o b

→ → →

Words I Can Read

where

is

go

that

come

Sentences I Can Read

1. Where are Mom and Bud?

2. Mom is in the tent.

3. Bud did not go with Mom.

4. Bud is at that spot with Dad.

5. They will come in at six.

Phonics

I Can Read!

Decodable Reader

● Short *Aa*

Ann	Cass	sad
ham	pan	pass
can	yam	jam
tan		

■ Short *Ii*

sit	Kim	did
will	miss	it
big	in	fix
mix	dip	fill
grin	sit	

▲ Short *Oo*

Tom	Jon	got
not	hot	pot

★ High-Frequency Words

where	go
is	a
the	that
with	

♥ Read the story.

Will Cass Come?

Written by Tracy Hawks
Illustrated by Bill Pars

Decodable Reader
32

Sit, Tom. Sit, Kim.
Sit, Ann. Sit, Jon.

Where did Cass go?
Cass will miss it.
Cass is sad.

Tom got a big ham.
Ham is in a big pan.
Pass us ham, Tom.

Ann can fix a yam.
It is not hot.
Pass us the yam, Ann.

Jon can mix dip.
Dip will fill that pan.
Pass us dip, Jon.

Kim can come with red jam.
Jam is in a tan pot.
Pass us red jam, Kim.

It is Cass!

Cass can grin.

Cass can sit with us.

Objectives
● Point out parts of a story including the characters. ● Tell in your own words a main event from a story read aloud. ● Describe characters in a story and why they act the way they do.
● Connect what you read to your own experiences.

Envision It! | Retell

Trade Book

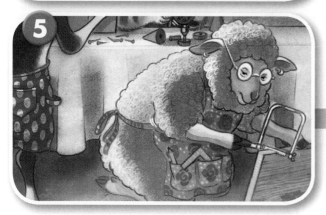

READING STREET ONLINE
STORY SORT
www.ReadingStreet.com

Think, Talk, and Write

1. Which tools have you seen someone use? **Text to Self**

2. Which is a character from *Old MacDonald had a Woodshop*? What does she do in the story? **Character**

3. Look back and write.

Objectives
● Understand and use new words that name places. ● Listen closely to speakers by facing them and asking questions to help you better understand the information. ● Share information and ideas by speaking clearly and using proper language.

Let's Learn It!

Vocabulary

● Talk about the pictures.

■ Where do you go if you want to ride a train?

▲ Where do firefighters work? police officers?

★ Where do you go if you need gas for your car?

Listening and Speaking

● Put your thumb up when you hear a fact.

■ Put your thumb down when you hear an opinion.

Vocabulary

Location Words

train station

police station

fire station

gas station

Discuss Fact and Opinion

Be a good listener!

49

Objectives

● Point out the details in stories that appeal to your five senses. ● Point out the phrases that appear in many stories from around the world.
● Respond to rhythm and rhyme in poetry by pointing out the beats and the rhyming words.

Let's
Practice
It!

Lullaby

● Listen to the lullaby.

■ Clap your hands to show the beats.

▲ What line is repeated four times?

★ To whom is the lullaby sung? Why?

♥ What does the lambs' fleece look and feel like?

Sleep, Baby, Sleep

Objectives
- Point out groups of spoken words that begin with the same sound.
- Segment words with one syllable into two to three sounds.

Let's Listen for

Read Together

Vowel Sounds

● Point to an elf. Say *elf*. Say the beginning sound.

■ Point to the bed. Say *bed*. Say the middle sound.

▲ Find three things that begin with /e/, like *elf*. Find three things that have /e/ in the middle, like *bed*.

★ Point to these pictures and say the words: *elephant, net, elbow*. Do they begin the same? What about *elk, elevator, egg*?

♥ Point to the bed. What sounds do you hear in *bed*? Separate the sounds with me: /b/ /e/ /d/.

READING STREET ONLINE
BIG QUESTION VIDEO
www.ReadingStreet.com

Envision It!

Main Idea

READING STREET ONLINE
ENVISION IT! ANIMATIONS
www.ReadingStreet.com

School

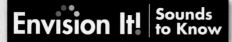

Ee

escalator

Phonics

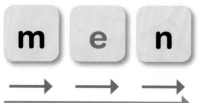 **Short e**

Words I Can Blend

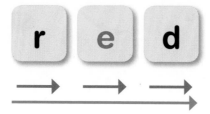

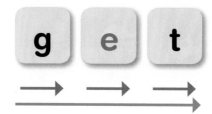

m e n → → →

r e d → → →

g e t → → →

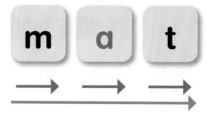

m a t → → →

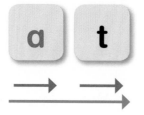

a t → →

Words I Can Read

the

was

to

like

from

Sentences I Can Read

1. The man had a big pet.

2. The pet was a tan dog.

3. The dog went to run.

4. Dogs like to run.

5. Dogs run from big cats.

Objectives
● Point out the common sounds that letters stand for. ● Use what you know about letters and their sounds to read words in a list and in sentences or stories. ● Know and read at least 25 often-used words.

Phonics

I Can Read!

Decodable Reader

● Short *Aa*
mat   sat   can
pass   add   ham
and

■ Short *Ee*
Ed   red   hen
egg   set   bed
well   net

▲ Short *Ii*
big   in   it
tin   Tim   grin

★ Short *Oo*
got   on   hop
toss   pot

♥ High-Frequency Words
a   the   what
do   with   to

◆ Read the story.

READING STREET ONLINE
DECODABLE eREADERS
www.ReadingStreet.com

Decodable Reader 33

The Red Egg
Written by Robert Smith
Illustrated by Perry Scott

Ed got a big,
red hen egg.
Ed set the egg on a mat.

Ed sat on the bed.
What can Ed do
with the red egg?

Ed can hop well
with the red egg.
Hop, Ed, hop.

Ed can toss the red egg
in a big net.
Toss it, Ed.

Ed can pass the red egg
in a tin can.
Pass it, Ed.

Ed can set the red egg
in a big pot.
Set it, Ed.

Ed can add ham
to the big, red hen egg.
Ed and Tim can grin.

Big Book

Envision It! Retell

Think, Talk, and Write

1. What does a beaver use to cut down trees and build its house? **Text to World**

2. What is the story *Building Beavers* mostly about?

Main Idea

3. Look back and write.

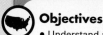

Objectives
• Understand and use new words that name actions, directions, positions, the order of something, and places. • Tell the meaning of signs. • Listen closely to speakers by facing them and asking questions to help you better understand the information.

Let's Learn It!

Vocabulary

● Talk about the pictures.

■ Which actions can you do?

Listening and Speaking

● Point to Sign 1. What do you do when you see this sign?

■ Point to Sign 2. What does this sign mean?

▲ Point to Sign 3. What does this sign mean?

Vocabulary

Words for Actions

dig

carry

eat

sleep

Interpret Information

1.

2.

3.

Get Ready For Grade 1

Be a good listener!

The Milkmaid and Her Pail

Let's Practice It!

Fable

● Listen to the fable.

■ What happens to the pail of milk? What does this do to the milkmaid's plan to get a new dress?

▲ Tell in your own words what the moral means.

★ Why do people listen to or read fables?

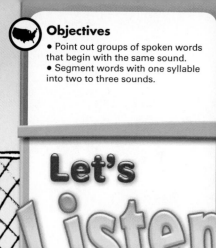

Objectives
● Point out groups of spoken words that begin with the same sound.
● Segment words with one syllable into two to three sounds.

Let's Listen for

Vowel Sounds

Read Together

● Point to the up arrow. Say *up*. Say the beginning sound.

■ Point to the sun. Say *sun*. Say the middle sound.

▲ Find three things that begin with /u/, like *up*. Find three things that have /u/ in the middle, like *sun*.

★ Say these words: *umbrella, up, ax*. Do they begin the same? What about *up, umpire, under*?

♥ Point to *up*. What sounds do you hear in *up*? Separate the sounds with me: /u/ /p/.

READING STREET ONLINE
BIG QUESTION VIDEO
www.ReadingStreet.com

Objectives

• Point out parts of a story including where it takes place, the characters, and the main events.

Comprehension

Envision It!

Literary Elements

READING STREET ONLINE
ENVISION IT! ANIMATIONS
www.ReadingStreet.com

Characters

Setting

Plot

Objectives
● Notice that new words are made when letters are changed, added, or taken away. ● Know and read at least 25 often-used words.

Envision It! | **Sounds to Know**

Uu

umbrella

READING STREET ONLINE
ALPHABET CARDS
www.ReadingStreet.com

Phonics

 Short *u*

Words I Can Blend

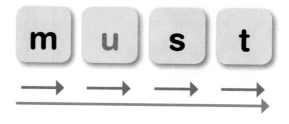

m u s t

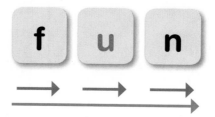

f u n

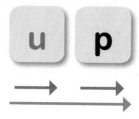

u p

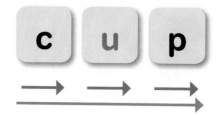

c u p

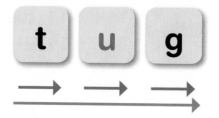

t u g

76

Words I Can Read

for

my

of

we

yellow

Sentences I Can Read

1. That gift is for me.
2. My mom got it for me.
3. It is a big box of hats.
4. We like to dress up.
5. The yellow hat is best.

Phonics

I Can Read!

Decodable Reader

● Short *Aa*

can	fast
lap	had

■ Short *Ee*

pet

▲ Short *Ii*

big	will	hill
dig	in	did
sip	if	it
sit		

★ Short *Oo*

Spot	not	lot
hot	on	top

♥ Short *Uu*

pup	run	fun
up	mud	tug
hug	jump	

◆ High-Frequency Words

is	my	a
for	the	of
I	with	what
we		

❋ Read the story.

Fun with Spot

Decodable Reader
34

Written by Cassandra Belton
Illustrated by Joseph Green

Spot is my pup.
Spot is not a big pet.

Spot can run fast.
Spot will run for fun.
Spot will run up the hill.

Spot can dig.
Spot will dig in the mud.
Spot will dig up a lot of mud.

Spot can tug.
I will tug with Spot.
What did Spot tug?

Spot can sip.
If it is hot,
Spot will sip a lot.

Spot can sit.
Spot will sit on my lap
on top of the hill.

I will hug Spot.
Spot had fun.
We will jump up.

Objectives
- Point out parts of a story including where it takes place, the characters, and the main events.
- Retell or act out important events of a story.
- Connect what you read to other things you have read or heard.

Envision It! | Retell

Trade Book

1

2

3

4

5

6
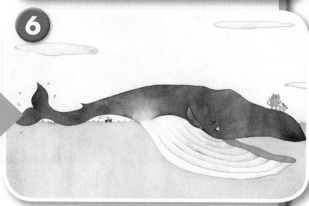

Think, Talk, and Write

1. How are Alistair and Kip like other friends we have read about? How are they different? Text to Text

2.

Beginning	
Middle	
End	

Choose an important part of the story. Act it out with some friends. ↻ Plot

3. Look back and write.

Objectives
- Understand and use new words that name actions, directions, positions, the order of something, and places.
- Listen closely to speakers by facing them and asking questions to help you better understand the information.

Let's Learn It!

Vocabulary

- Talk about the pictures.
- ■ Where can you go if you are hurt?
- ▲ Where can you go if you need food? money?
- ★ Where can you go to wash your clothes?

Listening and Speaking

- What do we learn about Max and Uncle Bunny in the story?
- ■ What do we learn about Ruby in the story?
- ▲ What events in the story show what Max, Uncle Bunny, and Ruby are like?

Location Words

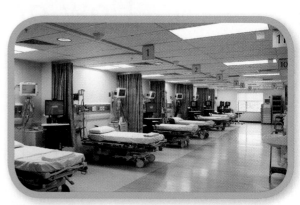

hospital

bank

grocery store

laundromat

Discuss Literary Elements
Character

Be a good listener!

Objectives
● Ask and answer questions about texts read aloud. ● Tell what an informational story read aloud was about. ● Tell the meaning of signs. ● Discuss the reasons for reading and listening to different kinds of texts.

Let's Practice It!

Signs

● Listen to the selection.

■ What is the selection about?

▲ Point to each sign. Tell what it means.

★ What do you notice about the shapes and colors of the signs?

♥ Why are traffic signs important?

✻ What questions do you have about these signs?

SCHOOL

RR

RR

LIBRARY

BOOKS

Objectives
● Say rhymes for words that are said to you. ● Blend spoken sounds to form words with one syllable. ● Say the sound at the beginning of spoken one-syllable words.

Phonemic Awareness

Let's Listen for

Read Together

Consonant and Vowel Sounds

● Point to the bat. Say the word. Say the beginning sound. Find two more things that begin with /b/.

■ Point to a cat. Say *cat*. Say the middle sound. Find two more things with /a/ in the middle.

▲ Blend /s/ /u/ /n/. What's the word? Yes, *sun*. Point to the picture.

★ What is the last sound in *sun*? Point to two more things that end with /n/, like *sun*.

♥ Say *mug*. Name two things that rhyme with *mug*.

READING STREET ONLINE
BIG QUESTION VIDEO
www.ReadingStreet.com

92

Comprehension

Envision It!

Literary Elements

**READING STREET ONLINE
ENVISION IT! ANIMATIONS**
www.ReadingStreet.com

Characters

Setting

Plot

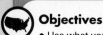
Phonics

🔊 Decode Words

Words I Can Blend

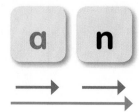

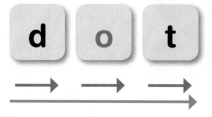

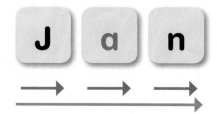

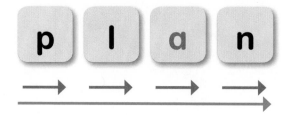

Words I Can Read

| have |
| they |
| two |
| four |
| blue |

Sentences I Can Read

1. We have a little plan.
2. They have a big plan.
3. We will get two to help.
4. They will get four.
5. Can we fill blue cups?

Objectives
● Point out the common sounds that letters stand for. ● Use what you know about letters and their sounds to read words in a list and in sentences or stories. ● Know and read at least 25 often-used words.

Phonics

I Can Read!

Decodable Reader

● Short *Aa*

Jan	tan	had
fat	an	bat
can		

■ Short *Ee*

red	net	wet
Deb	fed	Wes
hen	fell	egg
well		

▲ Short *Ii*

will	in	big
pig	Kim	slim
mitt	win	did
quit		

★ Short *Oo*

Todd	got	hot
Rob	not	

♥ Short *Uu*

fun	sun	mud
snug	run	

◆ High-Frequency Words

a	they
have	the

❋ Read the story.

READING STREET ONLINE
DECODABLE eREADERS
www.ReadingStreet.com

Fun in the Sun

Written by Harry Reynolds
Illustrated by Dan Vick

Decodable Reader 35

Todd got a red net.
Jan got a tan net.
Will they have fun?

Todd got wet.
Jan got wet.
They had fun in the hot sun!

Deb fed a big, fat pig.
Wes fed a red hen.
Will they have fun?

Deb fell in the mud.
Wes got an egg.
They had fun in the hot sun!

Kim got a slim bat.
Rob got a snug mitt.
Will they win?

Kim can run well. Kim did win.
Rob did not quit. Rob did win.

They had fun in the hot sun!

Objectives
● Point out parts of a story including where it takes place, the characters, and the main events. ● Tell in your own words a main event from a story read aloud.

Envision It! Retell

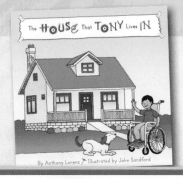

The HOUSE That TONY Lives IN

By Anthony Lorenz Illustrated by John Sandford

Big Book

READING STREET ONLINE
STORY SORT
www.ReadingStreet.com

Think, Talk, and Write

1. How does each one help build a house? **Text to World**

2. Where does the story *The House That Tony Lives In* take place? ○ Setting

3. Look back and write.

Objectives
● Listen closely to speakers by facing them and asking questions to help you better understand the information.
● Follow rules for discussions, including taking turns and speaking one at a time.

Let's Learn It!

Vocabulary

● Talk about the pictures.

■ Show you are frightened.

▲ When might you feel worried?

★ When might you feel proud?

♥ Show you are angry.

Listening and Speaking

● What is the title of the book?

■ Who is the author? Who is the illustrator?

▲ What is the setting of the story?

★ Tell what happens at the beginning, in the middle, and at the end of the story.

Vocabulary

Words for Feelings

frightened

worried

proud

angry

Oral Presentation
Book Report

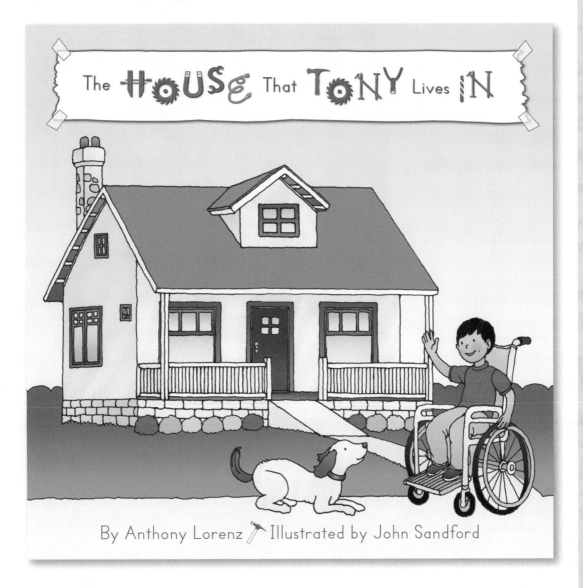

The HOUSE That TONY Lives IN

By Anthony Lorenz Illustrated by John Sandford

Be a good speaker!

Juan Bobo

Let's Practice It!

Folk Tale

● Listen to the folk tale.

■ How does it begin?

▲ Why does Juan Bobo put the burro on his shoulder?

★ Juan Bobo is a character in many Hispanic folk tales. Why do you think this is so?

♥ What can you learn from Juan Bobo?

Objectives
• Point out groups of spoken words that begin with the same sound.
• Say the sound at the beginning of spoken one-syllable words.

Phonemic Awareness

Let's Listen for

Blends

● Point to the broom. Say the word. Say the beginning blend. Find two more things that begin with /br/.

■ Point to the limb. Say *limb*. Say the middle sound. Find two more things with /i/ in the middle.

▲ Point to a plant. Say the word. Say the blend you hear at the end. Find two more things that end with /nt/.

★ Point to these pictures and say the words: *brown, bricks, brush.* Do they begin the same? What about *drink, sticks, broom?*

READING STREET ONLINE
BIG QUESTION VIDEO
www.ReadingStreet.com

Read Together

Comprehension

Envision It!

Draw Conclusions

READING STREET ONLINE
ENVISION IT! ANIMATIONS
www.ReadingStreet.com

Happy Happy Happy Happy Happy Happy

Envision It! | **Sounds to Know**

Yy

yo-yo

Ss

salamander

Phonics

Decode Words

Words I Can Blend

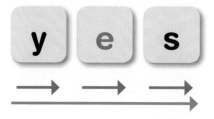

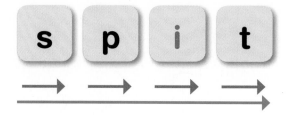

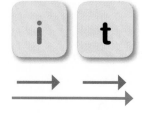

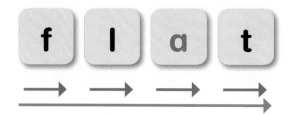

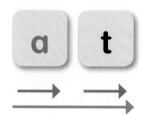

Words I Can Read

you

see

said

look

three

Sentences I Can Read

1. Do you see that?

2. "They are fast," said Dad.

3. "Look at the pups!" I said.

4. "I see three," Dad said.

5. Can I have a pup, Dad?

Objectives
• Point out the common sounds that letters stand for. • Use what you know about letters and their sounds to read words in a list and in sentences or stories. • Know and read at least 25 often-used words.

Phonics

I Can Read!

Decodable Reader

● Short *Aa*

an	Pam	Cat
can	had	tan
fan	flat	pan
ham	bad	

■ Short *Ee*

yes	let	bed
red	fed	

▲ Short *Ii*

big	did	in
it	sit	

★ Short *Oo*

odd	box	Tom
Fox	on	hot
not		

♥ Short *Uu*

jump	yum	fun

◆ High-Frequency Words

what	said	I
see	you	the
a	with	they
for		

✽ Read the story.

**READING STREET ONLINE
DECODABLE eREADERS**
www.ReadingStreet.com

The Box

Written by Andrea Brooks
Illustrated by Linda Bird

Decodable Reader 36

"What an odd, big box!"
Pam Cat said.
"Can I see?"

"Yes, you can," said Tom Fox.
Tom Fox did let Pam Cat
see in the box.

Tom Fox had a tan bed
in the big box.
Tom Fox can jump on it.

Tom Fox had a red fan
in the big box.
Tom Fox can sit with the fan on.

Tom Fox had a flat pan
in the big box.
Tom Fox fed Pam Cat hot ham.

123

Pam Cat had hot ham
with Tom Fox.
Yum, yum! They had fun.

"Not bad for
an odd, big box,"
Pam Cat said.

Objectives
● Retell the important facts from a selection heard or read.
● Connect what you read to your own experiences, to other things you have read or heard, and to the world around you.

Trade Book

Envision It! | Retell

Think, Talk, and Write

1. How are beavers and the way they build their homes like ants and the way they build their nests? **Text to Text**

2. Think about what **sticky** means. Why do you think ants use sticky silk to build their nests? **Draw Conclusions**

3. Look back and write.

Objectives
● Follow rules for discussions, including taking turns and speaking one at a time.

Let's Learn It!

Vocabulary

● Talk about the pictures.

■ Which bugs have wings?

▲ Which bugs have you seen?

Listening and Speaking

● Where does the story take place?

■ During what season does the story take place?

▲ Why doesn't the story take place in the desert?

Vocabulary

Words for Bugs

ant

bee

fly

spider

Discuss Literary Elements
Setting

Be a good listener!

A Man at a Restaurant in Crewe

Let's Practice It!

①

Poem

- ● Listen to the poem.
- ■ Clap your hands to show the beats.
- ▲ Which words rhyme?
- ★ Do you think the poem is funny? Why or why not?
- ♥ Why do people like to listen to or read this kind of poem?

Words for Things That Go

airplane

bike

truck

car

bus

van

boat

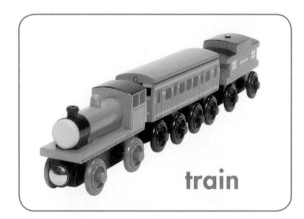

train

Words for Colors

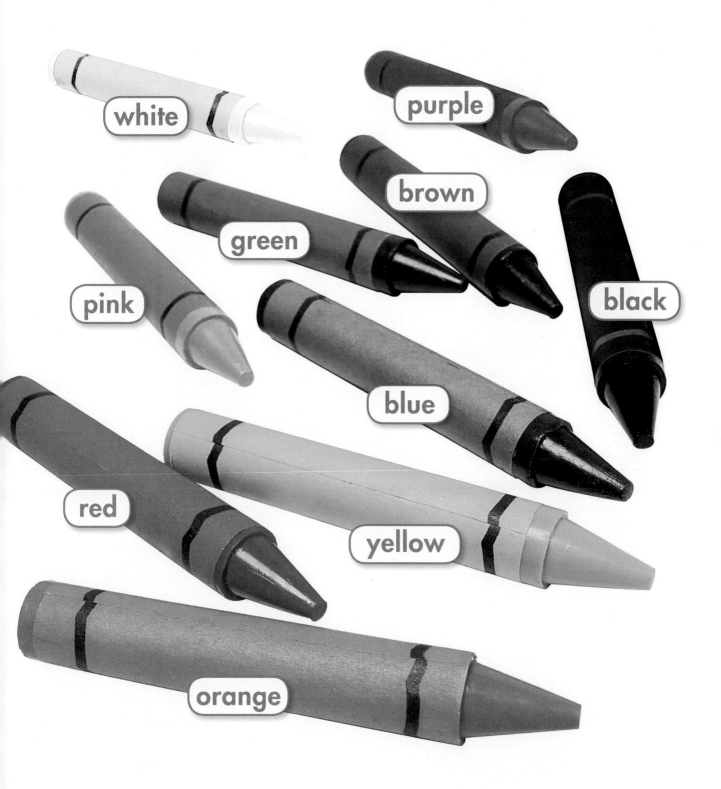

white

purple

brown

green

black

pink

blue

red

yellow

orange

Words for Shapes

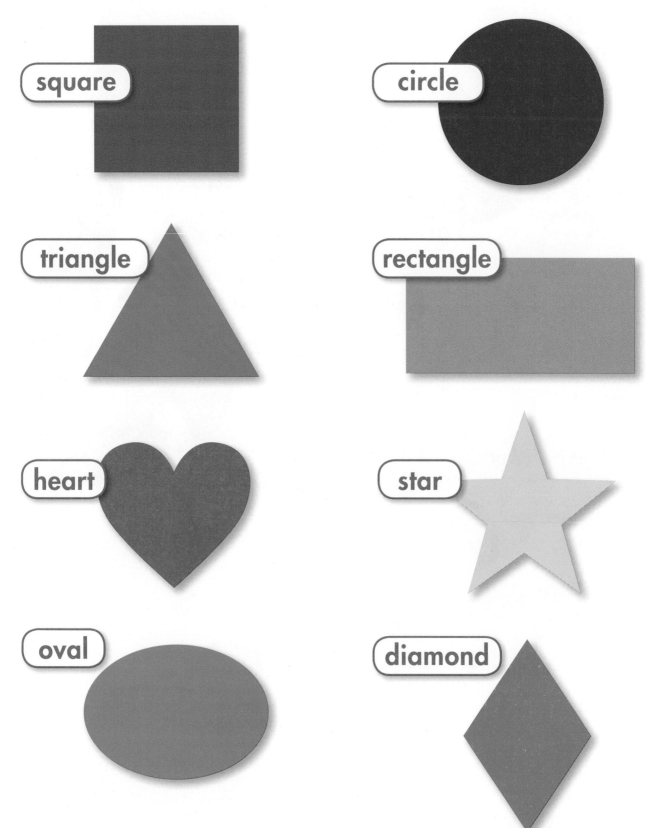

square

circle

triangle

rectangle

heart

star

oval

diamond

Words for Places

school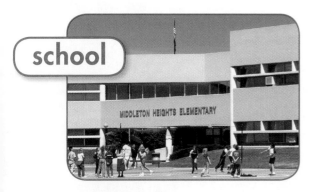

home

park

train station

police station

fire station

post office

library

Words for Animals

lion

mouse

puppy

dog

cat

duck

turtle

kitten

chick

hen

rooster

bird

butterfly

fish

whale

caterpillar

bear

panda

beaver

calf

cow

Words for Actions

skip

walk

run

fly

swim

ride

jump

hop

Position Words

up

in

out

down

on

around

over

under

My Classroom

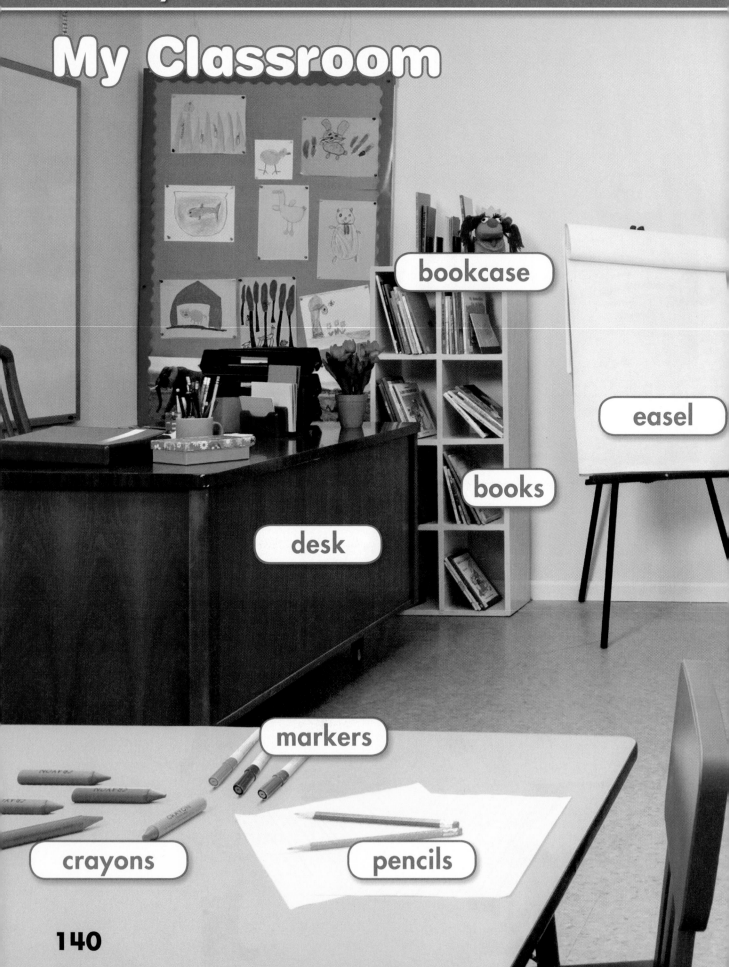

bookcase

easel

books

desk

markers

crayons

pencils

teacher

toys

paper

chair

blocks

table

rug

Words for Feelings

happy

frightened

worried

excited

angry

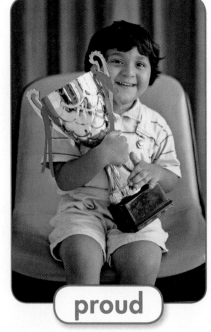

proud

sad

surprised

My Family

mom
mother

dad
father

sister

grandmother

grandfather

brother

Acknowledgments

Illustrations

Cover: Rob Hefferan

12 Amanda Haley

28–29, 49, 68, 108, 112 Anthony Lewis

32 Jannie Ho

39–45 Natalia Vasquez

50 Karen Stormer Brooks

52 Ron Lieser

59–65 Maria Mola

70–71 Martha Aviles

72 Stephen Lewis

79–85 Cale Atkinson

90 Ivanke & Lola

92 Jamie Smith

99–105 Dani Jones

110–111 Constanza Basaluzzo

119–125 Robbie Short

130–131 Cecilia Rebora.

Photographs

Every effort has been made to secure permission and provide appropriate credit for photographic material. The publisher deeply regrets any omission and pledges to correct errors called to its attention in subsequent editions.

Unless otherwise acknowledged, all photographs are the property of Pearson Education, Inc.

Photo locators denoted as follows: Top (T), Center (C), Bottom (B), Left (L), Right (R), Background (Bkgd)

10 (B) ©Ralf Gerard/Getty Images

30 (T) ©Digital Focus/Alamy

31 (T) ©Royalty-Free/Corbis

48 ©David R. Frazier Photolibrary, Inc./Alamy Images, ©Enigma/Alamy Images, ©Visions of America, LLC/Alamy Images

88 ©David Young-Wolff/PhotoEdit, Inc., ©Jeff Greenberg/Alamy Images, ©Tim Mantoani/Masterfile Corporation, ©Blend Images/Jupiter Images

128 Frank Greenaway/©DK Images, Geoff Brightling/©DK Images, Tim Ridley/©DK Images.